GALE

CENGAGE Learning

Novels for Students, Volume 33

Project Editor: Sara Constantakis Rights Acquisition and Management: Leitha Etheridge-Sims, Kelly Quin, Tracie Richardson, Mardell Glinski Schultz Composition: Evi Abou-El-Seoud Manufacturing: Drew Kalasky

Imaging: John Watkins

Product Design: Pamela A. E. Galbreath, Jennifer Wahi Content Conversion: Katrina Coach Product Manager: Meggin Condino © 2010 Gale, Cengage

For product information and technology assistance, contact us at **Gale Customer Support, 1-800-877-4253.**

For permission to use material from this text or product, submit all requests online at **www.cengage.com/permissions.**

Further permissions questions can be emailed to **permissionrequest@cengage.com** While every effort has been made to ensure the reliability of the information presented in this publication, Gale, a part of Cengage Learning, does not guarantee the accuracy of the data contained herein. Gale accepts no payment for listing; and inclusion in the publication of any organization, agency, institution, publication, service, or individual does not imply endorsement of the editors or publisher. Errors brought to the attention of the publisher and verified to the satisfaction of the publisher will be corrected in future editions.

Gale
27500 Drake Rd.
Farmington Hills, MI, 48331-3535

ISBN-13: 978-1-4144-4171-9
ISBN-10: 1-4144-4171-1
ISSN 1094-3552

This title is also available as an e-book.
ISBN-13: 978-1-4144-4949-4

ISBN-10: 1-4144-4949-6

Contact your Gale, a part of Cengage Learning sales representative for ordering information.

Printed in the United States of America
1 2 3 4 5 6 7 14 13 12 11 10

Kidnapped

Robert Louis Stevenson 1886

Introduction

Robert Louis Stevenson's *Kidnapped* (1886) is widely regarded as one of the finest boys' adventure novels ever written, although it is often overshadowed by the author's other major adventure tale, *Treasure Island* (1883). Still, many critics and scholars have agreed with Stevenson himself that the novel is, as he wrote in a letter to his father, "a far better story and far sounder at heart than *Treasure Island*."

Stevenson was inspired to write *Kidnapped* after researching an important murder trial that took place in Scotland in 1752—the Appin Murder, which figures prominently in the plot of the book. The novel tells the story of David Balfour, a poor Scottish teen who discovers upon his father's death that he is actually the heir to a wealthy estate. Before he can claim it, however, his greedy uncle has the boy kidnapped by sailors and taken to sea, to be sold into slavery in the American Colonies. The novel weaves fiction with the significant historical events of the time and includes detailed descriptions of various Scottish locales Stevenson had visited during his youth. Although the novel contains a great deal of phonetically rendered Scottish dialect and words specific to the region, the compelling story has helped the book remain a favorite among young readers for more than a century.

Author Biography

Stevenson was born on November 13, 1850, in Edinburgh, Scotland, the son of a lighthouse engineer. He was an only child, and suffered from illnesses made worse by the damp weather and air pollution in their ever-expanding capital city. Much of his youth was spent reading books, although he also enjoyed exploring the outdoors when his health allowed. He worked briefly with his father as an engineer in training. Although he was not consistently healthy enough to make it a career, this period of travel with his father opened his eyes to many new places such as Erraid, the Scottish tidal island on which David Balfour becomes shipwrecked in *Kidnapped*.

Stevenson went to law school to please his father but never actually practiced law, preferring instead to write. His first books mainly concerned his travels, and are considered among the first and finest examples of what came to be called the travelogue. In *Travels with a Donkey in the Cévennes* (1879), Stevenson wrote not only of the sights he saw, but also the history of the region and the sharp divide between Catholic and Protestant cultures—elements that would appear throughout much of his work, especially *Kidnapped*.

While traveling, he met and later married Fanny Osbourne, a woman from California with a young son named Lloyd. One day he and Lloyd began playfully creating a treasure map that showed the location of a pirate's gold. This eventually grew into Stevenson's first truly popular work and his first novel, *Treasure Island*. This marked the start of a creative period in which he produced his best-known works, including *Kidnapped, Strange Case of Dr. Jekyll and Mr. Hyde* (1886), and *The Master of Ballantrae* (1889).

In 1890, Stevenson moved to the Samoan Islands with the hope that the climate there would ease his still-chronic illnesses. He continued writing, and even produced a sequel to *Kidnapped* called *Catriona* (published in America as *David Balfour*) in 1893. However, both he and his readers found these books less compelling than his earlier works. Stevenson died of a stroke on December 3, 1894, at the age of forty-four.

Plot Summary

Chapters 1-4

Kidnapped begins in June of 1751, in a region of Scotland known as the Lowlands. David Balfour, an Essendean boy of sixteen, is left homeless when his seemingly poor schoolmaster father dies. With his mother already dead, David believes himself to be without inheritance or living relative until the local minister, Mister Campbell, gives him a letter prepared by David's father before his death. A note instructs David to take the letter to his heretofore unknown uncle, Ebenezer Balfour, at the house of Shaws in Cramond. The discovery that he hails from a wealthy family excites David, although Mister Campbell quickly reminds the boy—who has learned only simple country manners—to be on his best behavior when he arrives there. Mister Campbell gives David a Bible, a small amount of money, and a recipe for a healing drink, and David sets off on a two-day journey by foot to Cramond.

Along the way, David sees a regiment of the king's soldiers, known as "redcoats," marching past, and the sight fills him with pride. When he reaches the parish of Cramond, he asks local residents for directions to the Shaw house. He receives reactions both puzzled and negative, and begins to suspect that his family name and fortune may not be as grand as he had at first believed. When he finally arrives at the house of Shaws, he finds that "the house itself appeared to be a kind of ruin; no road led up to it; no smoke arose from any of the chimneys; nor was there any semblance of a garden." Indeed, the house seems unfinished, with exposed rooms on the upper floor and windows without glass.

Media Adaptations

- A filmed adaptation of the novel was released by Walt Disney Pictures in 1960. Perhaps the most acclaimed film adaptation of the book, this version, starring Peter Finch, Peter O'Toole, and James MacArthur, is currently available on DVD.

- A film adaptation was directed by Delbert Mann for Omnibus-American International in 1971. The film, which combines elements from both *Kidnapped* and its sequel, *Catriona*, stars Michael Caine and Donald Pleasance, among others. The film is not currently available in the United States.

- A made-for-television adaptation of the book was directed by Ivan Passer in 1995. This version, starring Armand Assante and Brian McCardie, is currently available on DVD.

- A film adaptation of the novel was directed by Brendan Maher for BBC in 2005. This version, starring Iain Glenn and James Pearson, combines the first novel with its sequel, *Catriona*. It is currently available on DVD.

- An unabridged audio adaptation of *Kidnapped* was released on CD by Brilliance Audio in 2001. The book is read by Michael Page.

- An unabridged audiobook version of *Kidnapped* was released on CD by Monterey Soundworks in 2002. The work features a theatrical presentation of the book text, including music and sound effects.

- An unabridged audio adaptation of the book was released on CD by Commuters Library in 2002. The book is read by Ralph Cosham.

- An unabridged audio version of the book was released in MP3 format by In Audio in 2003. The files are stored on audio CD, but can only be played in a player that recognizes MP3 audio files.

- An audio adaptation of the novel was released on CD by Edcon Publishing Group in 2008.

- An unabridged audio version of the novel was released on CD by Audio Book Contractors Inc. in 2008. The book is read by Flo Gibson.

- *Kidnapped* was adapted as a short graphic novel by Alan Grant and Cam Kennedy in 2007 as part of a celebration of Edinburgh's selection as the first UNESCO City of Literature.

- The novel was adapted as a five-issue comic book series by Roy Thomas and Mario Gully, and released under the *Marvel Illustrated* imprint in 2009.

After nightfall, David summons the courage to knock at the door, and is reluctantly greeted by an old man holding a gun. When the old man, Ebenezer Balfour, learns of David's identity—and presumably the death of his own brother—he agrees to let David inside. After a small meal of porridge, Ebenezer shows David to a bedroom, which the old man then locks from the outside. The next day, their relationship seems to improve slightly, and Ebenezer gives David thirty-seven gold guineas, each equal to one British pound, to fulfill a promise he says he once made to David's father. That evening, Ebenezer asks David to retrieve some papers from a trunk at the top of a tower several stories high. He sends David on the errand without so much as a candle to see by, and thanks only to the lightning from an approaching storm, the boy realizes that the staircase ends abruptly in front of him, high above the ground. After he safely climbs down, David accuses his uncle of trying to murder him and demands an explanation. The old man, surprised to see David still alive, falls victim to a weak heart and must lie down, although he promises to explain everything to David in the morning. David locks Ebenezer inside his room, just as Ebenezer had done to him the night before.

Chapters 5-8

The next morning, before Ebenezer explains himself—David assumes that "he had no lie ready for me, though he was hard at work preparing one"—a cabin boy knocks on the door with a letter for Ebenezer from his captain, Elias Hoseason. Ebenezer suggests to David that they go into the nearby port town of Queensferry, where Ebenezer can conduct business with the captain; after completing his business, he vows to take David to Mr. Rankeillor, a local lawyer, and straighten out matters of the boy's inheritance. David agrees, assuming the old man can do him no harm in such a public place.

The trio reaches Queensferry and meets Captain Hoseason at the local inn. David leaves the two older men alone to talk business, and while speaking with the landlord of the inn, David learns that his own father, Alexander, was actually the older brother of Ebenezer—contrary to what Ebenezer had claimed. From this, David realizes that he himself is the lawful heir to the entire family estate. Captain Hoseason and Ebenezer complete their business and the captain calls for David to join him briefly aboard his ship, the *Covenant*. David is wary to leave the safety of land in the company of one of his uncle's associates, but eventually he agrees. The captain, Ebenezer, and David board a rowboat and make their way to where the *Covenant* is anchored. Once David is aboard the ship, Ebenezer slips away and heads back toward shore. David realizes he has been betrayed and cries out for help, but he is struck from behind and knocked unconscious.

When David awakens, he finds himself tied up somewhere within the "ill-smelling cavern of the ship's bowels." He is visited by one of the captain's senior officers, Mr. Riach, who seems kind toward David and convinces the captain that the boy might die if he is left in such dismal conditions below decks. David is moved to the upper deck at the front of the ship, where he enjoys both sunlight and the company of the rough men who make up the ship's crew. David eventually pieces together his fate: he is to be taken to the Carolinas in the American Colonies, where he will be sold into slavery as part of Ebenezer's plan to keep the boy far away from his rightful claim on the family estate. Mr. Riach, whose kindness toward David appears only after he has been drinking, agrees to try and help the boy if he can.

Meanwhile, the cabin boy, Ransome, periodically relates to David terrible tales of his abuse at the hands of another of the ship's senior officers, Mr. Shuan. One night, David learns that Ransome has been severely beaten by Mr. Shuan; the boy is brought down to David's berth, and Captain Hoseason tells David that he is moving to the ship's roundhouse (a cabin that has one curved wall), where he will live and serve as the new cabin boy. Soon after, David hears that Ransome has died. The captain tells his officers that they will say the boy went overboard. Mr. Shuan changes starkly after the incident, becoming fearful of David and forgetful of Ransome's existence, as if the whole affair were just a nightmare. Despite this, and despite Mr. Riach's failure to deliver on his promise to help David return home, the boy settles rather easily into his new life aboard the ship.

Chapters 9-13

More than a week later, as David is serving

Captain Hoseason and Mr. Riach their supper, the *Covenant* strikes another, smaller vessel in the fog and sinks it. By good fortune and brute strength, one member of the smaller boat manages to grab onto the *Covenant* and climb aboard. They bring the man into the roundhouse for a meal and a drink. The man, short and weathered but wearing fine French clothes and carrying a belt filled with gold coins, explains that he is a fugitive in his native Scotland. He tells the captain that he works in the service of a Highland chief who has been exiled by King George, and who is the rightful heir to the throne of England, Ireland, and Scotland. The money he carries is rent paid by the chief's still-loyal clan members. If he is discovered by the king's soldiers, the redcoats, he will surely be imprisoned or killed.

Captain Hoseason refuses to transport the man to France, but agrees to take him as far as Linnhe Loch on the west coast of the Scottish Highlands in exchange for sixty gold guineas. The captain steps out with his officers, and David later overhears him planning to murder the man. They ask David to retrieve some pistols and gunpowder from the roundhouse, since most of the ship's weaponry is stored there and they do not want to raise the Highlander's suspicions by doing it themselves. David agrees, and returns to the roundhouse.

Instead of helping the captain and his men, David tells the Highlander, whose name is Alan Breck Stewart, of the captain's plot. Alan asks David to stand with him against the attackers, and

David agrees. They secure the roundhouse and load as many guns as possible before the captain and his men have a chance to advance. Although they are outnumbered fifteen to two, David and Alan successfully fend off their attackers, killing several of the crewmen. Alan is so impressed with David's courage that he gives the boy one of the silver buttons from his coat, which were given to him by his own father.

David learns of Alan's hatred for a man named Colin Roy Campbell, also known as the Red Fox, from a Scottish Highland clan that supported King George and made enemies of other Highland clans. Colin Roy was chosen as the king's agent in the area, and was responsible for seizing possession of the Stewart clan's estates in the name of the king. David also learns that Alan once served in the English army as a redcoat, but changed sides when his conscience got the better of him. For this act of desertion, capture by the redcoats would mean certain death for Alan.

Captain Hoseason eventually calls for a truce so that David and Alan can help the short-handed crew navigate the *Covenant* through treacherous waters off the western coast of Scotland. Despite their best efforts, the ship crashes into a reef and David is thrown overboard. He manages to make it to shore, but can find no sign of the rest of the crew or Alan.

Chapters 14-16

David explores the beach and surrounding area where he has washed ashore, and comes to the conclusion that he is trapped on an island with very little food or water available. He sees signs of a town on the main island of Mull across the strait from his island, and notes that "it seemed impossible that I should be left to die on the shores of my own country, and within view of a church tower and the smoke of men's houses." After four miserable days, David realizes that the body of water separating him from the main island all but disappears when the tide goes out, and that he can walk the distance without trouble.

David makes his way to the town he had seen from his previous location. He comes across an old gentleman who confirms that Alan and some of the other crewmen are still alive, and delivers a message: David is to travel to Torosay on the other side of the island, where he can then ferry to the mainland and meet up with Alan. The old gentleman and his wife offer David food and drink, and the man gives David a hat to wear on his journey.

At the end of the next day, David stops at another house and offers the poor man who lives there five shillings to let him stay the night and to guide David the following morning to Torosay. The man agrees, and after some delays caused by exchanging one of David's few remaining guineas for the smaller currency of shillings, they set off toward Torosay. The guide takes David part of the way, but demands more money to complete the journey. David agrees at first, but when the guide stops and asks for more money a second time, the two argue and the guide pulls a knife from his sleeve. David disarms the man and steals his knife and his shoes, and then continues on his way alone.

David soon encounters another traveler, a blind man who claims to be a man of religion. David is impressed by his ability to describe the nearby landmarks despite his lack of sight; as they walk, David realizes that the man carries a pistol and is acting suspiciously, and David threatens to shoot the man if he doesn't leave him alone. Upon arriving in Torosay, David discovers from a local innkeeper that the blind man is Duncan Mackiegh, known for being able to shoot accurately simply by sound, and also suspected of robbery and murder.

David takes the ferry from Torosay to Kinlochaline on the mainland. David shows the captain of the ferry, Neil Roy Macrob, his silver button from Alan's coat, and Neil delivers a message outlining the route David should take to reach the home of James of the Glens in Appin, where Alan will wait in safety among his clan. David spends the night at the inn at Kinlochaline, which he calls "the most beggarly vile place that pigs were ever styed in, full of smoke, vermin, and silent Highlanders."

The next morning, he sets out along the course Alan provided. He meets Henderland, a teacher of religion far more genuine than his traveling companions on Mull. Henderland provides David an evenhanded account of the history of conflict between the Campbells and the other clans in the area. The man also provides David with a meal, a sermon, and a very small amount of money to help him on his journey.

Chapters 17-19

David receives transport from a fisherman across the loch to Appin, Alan Breck's homeland. While resting on the roadside, the Red Fox himself —Colin Roy Campbell—approaches on horseback with some trusted cohorts and a group of redcoats marching behind. David stops the man and asks him for directions to the home of James of the Glens. As the two converse, Campbell is shot dead. Campbell's associates accuse David of being an accomplice who stopped the group so that Campbell could be killed. David runs away, and runs into Alan Breck hiding nearby. After the two escape the king's agents and soldiers, David accuses Alan of being the murderer. Alan denies it, and David acknowledges seeing another man flee from the area after the shooting. However, Alan refuses to identify the shooter, and argues that it is better for the two of them to be suspected as the killers, since this would draw the soldiers away from the guilty man—who is surely a member of Alan's clan. Although David disagrees with his reasoning, he goes with Alan to the home of James of the Glens in an attempt to effect an escape for both Alan and himself.

James is greatly distressed by the killing of

Campbell, since he knows the blame will be put upon his people and his own family. He informs Alan that while he will help the two escape, he must also put out papers offering a reward for their capture. David is given a change of clothes so that his description will not match the one known to the king's men, and David and Alan set off for safer lands to the east of Appin.

Chapters 20-24

The two fugitives head eastward at a relentless pace, crossing mountains, rivers, and forests in an attempt to outrun the king's soldiers. At one point, they find themselves in the same open valley as a camp of redcoats, but the pair ultimately manages to escape unseen. They reach relative safety in a place called Corrynakiegh, and Alan uses the silver button he gave David to send a message to a friend who lives there, John Breck Maccoll. Maccoll relays a message to James of the Glens, and brings back to Alan and David a small amount of money, a copy of the paper describing them as fugitives, and news that James himself has been taken prisoner by the king's men.

The pair continues eastward until they reach the moors, a flat, open area where it is nearly impossible to hide from soldiers. They spy a group of soldiers on horseback headed their way from the east, and change course to the north to reach Ben Alder, a mountain that can provide cover. As they approach Ben Alder, they encounter the clansmen of Cluny Macpherson, a rebel against the king and fugitive himself. David and Alan are invited to stay with Cluny in his hideout.

David, exhausted from their travels, falls ill for two days as Alan spends time playing cards with Cluny. Alan wakes David at one point and borrows the boy's small amount of remaining money. When David fully recovers from his illness and the pair prepare to head southward, he discovers that Alan has lost all of their money—both his own and David's—playing cards. Cluny is kind enough to return David's portion of the money, leaving very little for both men to spend during their travels.

Alan apologizes to David for the incident, but David refuses to accept his apology. This leads to a quarrel that nearly ends in a sword fight, but Alan refuses to fight. David, growing ever weaker, finally tells Alan that he cannot continue onward without his friend's help, and with that, their friendship is restored.

Chapters 25-30

David and Alan make their way southeast across Balquidder, a region filled with as many potential enemies as friends. Luckily, they arrive first at a home where Alan is known by name and well regarded, and the family—of the Maclaren clan —allows David to recover there for nearly a month. During that time, David is visited by Robin Oig, outlaw son of Scottish folk hero Rob Roy Macgregor. Robin and Alan clash when they meet, and almost draw swords before the host of the house, Duncan Dhu, suggests that they instead resolve their conflict by playing pipes. Alan plays impressively, but Robin is a master piper, and clearly wins the contest. All ill feeling disappears when Alan admits, "It would go against my heart to haggle a man that can blow the pipes as you can!"

When David and Alan finally leave Balquidder, it is near the end of August. They continue southeast toward the Firth of Forth, the body of water where David had been kidnapped two months before. The town of Queensferry and the home of the lawyer, Mr. Rankeillor, who David hopes will help him reclaim his rightful inheritance, both lie just across the water. However, David and Alan are unable to cross by bridge, where they would encounter soldiers. Instead, they reach Limekilns and gain the sympathies of a local innkeeper's daughter. She agrees to help, and under cover of night she steals a neighbor's boat and rows them across the water. Before they even have a chance to thank her, she rows away.

The next day, David finds Mr. Rankeillor and tells the man his story. Although David's tale is difficult to believe, the story fits with the small amount of information Mr. Rankeillor has received. Between them, the two devise a plan to get Ebenezer to confess his part in the kidnapping. They enlist Alan to help, and he tricks Ebenezer into admitting that he paid Captain Hoseason twenty pounds to take David away to the Carolinas to be sold into slavery. Mr. Rankeillor, his assistant

Torrance, and David reveal themselves as witnesses to the admission, and Ebenezer agrees to pay David two-thirds of the yearly family income as his rightful inheritance.

With David's future secure, he and Alan head toward Edinburgh, where David plans to find a lawyer descended from the Appin Stewarts—and therefore trustworthy—to help Alan find a way out of the country. The two part ways, and Alan remains in hiding, awaiting David's further assistance. The story ends with David standing before his bank in Edinburgh, and concludes with an assurance from the author that from that point on, "whatever befell them, it was not dishonor, and whatever failed them, they were not found wanting to themselves."

Characters

David Balfour

The hero of *Kidnapped*, David Balfour is a sixteen-year-old boy from Essendean whose seemingly poor father, a schoolmaster, has just died. With his mother already dead, David has no choice but to leave the rented family home and find his way in the world. A letter left for him by his father sends him on a journey to Cramond, where he learns that he is actually from a wealthy family, the Shaws. An encounter with his devious uncle Ebenezer ends with David being kidnapped and taken aboard a ship bound for the American Colonies, where he will be sold into slavery. Aboard the ship, David meets Alan Breck Stewart and forms a friendship that keeps both of them alive through many perils, not the least of which include a shipwreck and being suspected of murdering a prominent agent of the king. David eventually returns to his rightful home, the estate of the Shaws, and claims his inheritance before departing for Edinburgh to help his friend Alan escape the country.

Ebenezer Balfour

The uncle of David Balfour, Ebenezer is the younger brother of David's father Alexander, rightful heir to the Shaws estate. As young men, the two quarreled over the love of a girl—David's mother—and Alexander gave up his claim to the Shaws estate in exchange for a life of happiness and family. Unfortunately, all the wealth of the house of Shaws could not make Ebenezer happy, and he became a bitter hermit within the ruined estate. His reputation among the locals of Cramond is poor, and his cruelty and greed have seriously tarnished the family name. When David shows up at his door, Ebenezer realizes that the only thing he has—his wealth—is in danger, since the estate belongs by law to Alexander and his descendants. He attempts to cause David to fall to his death while climbing an incomplete stairway, and when that ploy fails, he pays Captain Hoseason to kidnap the young man and take him to the Carolinas. After David returns and exposes Ebenezer's plan, Ebenezer agrees to give David the bulk of the estate.

Colin Roy Campbell

Campbell is a prominent member of a Scottish Highland clan who has become an agent of King George of England. His family's allegiance to the king has angered many other Highland clans, including the Stewart clan, of which Alan Breck Stewart is a member. A real-life historical figure, Campbell was entrusted with evicting the families of many Highland clans and taking control of their estates in the name of the king. In *Kidnapped*, David speaks briefly to Campbell and is a witness to his death by shooting—an actual historical event. In the novel, David and Alan Breck Stewart are accused of taking part in the murder.

Mister Campbell

The minister at Essendean, where David Balfour was raised, Mister Campbell is a close friend of David's father and looks after David until he leaves Essendean for Cramond. Mister Campbell is the one David's father entrusted to deliver a letter to David after his death; it is this letter that marks the beginning of David's adventures. Before David departs on his journey, Mister Campbell gives David some money, a Bible, and a recipe for Lily of the Valley water. Campbell also warns David of the temptations and dangers he may face along the way.

Jennet Clouston

A former tenant of Ebenezer Balfour, Jennet Clouston speaks with David on his journey to the house of Shaws. She has nothing good to say about Ebenezer, and says she has cursed him "twelve hunner and nineteen" times—according to Ebenezer, once for every day since he evicted her.

Mister Henderland

Mister Henderland is a religious teacher David meets while walking from Kinlochaline toward Appin. Henderland proves to be knowledgeable, fair-minded, and altogether pleasant traveling company for David. Henderland even invites David to stay at his house, offers him a small amount of money for his journey, and finds a fisherman to transport David across Linnhe Loch to Appin.

Elias Hoseason

Elias Hoseason is the captain of the ship *Covenant*, in the employ of Ebenezer Balfour. After David Balfour arrives at the house of Shaws, Ebenezer pays Hoseason twenty pounds to lure the boy to his ship, kidnap him, and sell him into slavery in the Carolinas. Hoseason later recruits David as his cabin boy aboard the *Covenant*. After David overhears Hoseason and his officers plotting to kill Alan Breck Stewart, he tells Alan and the two fend off the attackers. Hoseason eventually loses his beloved ship by crashing into a reef off the coast of Mull, but he survives.

Innkeeper at Queensferry

While in Queensferry for the first time, David speaks to an innkeeper who provides him valuable information about his father. David discovers from the innkeeper that his father was actually the older brother of Ebenezer, contrary to what Ebenezer had told him; this means that David, not Ebenezer, is the rightful heir to the house of Shaws.

Innkeeper's Daughter in Limekilns

In Limekilns, David and Alan encounter an innkeeper's daughter who proves instrumental in their safe passage to Queensferry. Unable to cross the Firth of Forth by bridge, the two must find a way across the water. They find an inn and play upon the sympathies of the innkeeper's daughter, telling her that David is likely to be killed if they cannot find someone to ferry them across the water. She agrees to help, and after nightfall she steals a boat and rows the pair across the water herself.

James of the Glens

See James Stewart

John Breck Maccoll

John Breck Maccoll is a good friend of Alan Breck Stewart's who lives in Koalisnacoan. When David and Alan are on the run as fugitives, Alan contacts John Breck and asks him to deliver a message to James Stewart. Although he initially refuses, John Breck delivers the message and returns to Alan and David with both some money and the information that James Stewart has been arrested by the king.

Duncan Mackiegh

Duncan Mackiegh is a blind religious instructor on the island of Mull. David encounters Mackiegh during his journey from Erraid to the ferry at Torosay. Although he is blind, he carries a silver pistol and can name every landmark along the road where he and David stand. While walking with Mackiegh, David grows to suspect that the man plans to harm or rob him, so he threatens Mackiegh and drives him away. David later discovers that Mackiegh, even though blind, is considered an excellent shot at close range, and is suspected of both robbery and murder.

Duncan Dhu Maclaren

Duncan Dhu Maclaren is a Balquidder resident whose family is friendly with the Stewart clan. David and Alan are fortunate enough to knock upon Duncan's door when David is ill and in need of help. The two remain in Duncan Dhu's home for nearly a month as David recovers, and Duncan frequently entertains everyone with his pipe-playing. When Robin Oig visits and a confrontation occurs between Oig and Alan, Duncan defuses the situation by asking them both to participate in a pipe-playing contest.

Cluny Macpherson

A Highland chief on the run from the British government, Cluny Macpherson hides out in a secret place near Ben Alder called "Cluny's Cage." David and Alan are brought to him by his men, who find the pair evading redcoats nearby. During their stay in Cluny's Cage, David is ill, but Alan keeps Cluny company by playing cards. Unfortunately, Alan loses all of his own money as well as David's. Cluny, being a gentleman, returns David's money.

Neil Roy Macrob

Neil Roy Macrob is the ferryman who transports David from Torosay to the mainland at Kinlochaline. Macrob is a friend of Alan Breck Stewart's, and after David shows him Alan's silver coat button, he gives David instructions for meeting Alan in Appin.

Robin Oig

Robin Oig is the son of Rob Roy, a legendary outlaw and hero to many Scots. Robin himself is also a fugitive from the law, having been part of a plot to kidnap a wealthy widow and force her to marry him. He meets David and Alan during their stay in Balquidder, and defeats Alan in a pipe-playing contest.

Mister Rankeillor

Mister Rankeillor is a lawyer in Queensferry familiar with the dealings between Ebenezer Balfour and his deceased brother, Alexander. Ebenezer promises to take David to see Rankeillor before having the boy kidnapped. When David returns from the Highlands, he finds Rankeillor and tells him what has transpired, including his uncle's devious plan. Rankeillor helps David get Ebenezer to admit his part in the kidnapping, and is instrumental in securing David's rightful inheritance.

Ransome

Ransome is the cabin boy aboard Captain Hoseason's ship, the *Covenant*. It is he who delivers a message from the captain to Ebenezer at the house of Shaws. David becomes somewhat friendly with Ransome while aboard the *Covenant*, and sees firsthand the abuse Ransome receives at the hands of Mr. Shuan. Ransome is eventually beaten to death by the drunken Mr. Shuan after offering the officer a dirty piece of dishware. Captain Hoseason and his officers agree to say that the boy simply fell overboard.

The Red Fox

See Colin Roy Campbell

Mister Riach

Mr. Riach is Captain Hoseason's second officer aboard the sailing ship *Covenant*. Riach is the one who knocks David unconscious after the young man boards the *Covenant*, and he later admits this freely to David. Riach's concern about David's well-being leads Hoseason to move the boy above-decks, where David's health improves. David later explains his situation to Riach, who agrees to help the boy return home. However, Riach never follows through on this promise, and is one of the crew members who attack David and Alan Breck Stewart after they block themselves in the roundhouse. David later learns that after the shipwreck, Riach takes arms against his fellow crewmen in an effort to protect Stewart from them.

Mister Shuan

Mr. Shuan is Captain Hoseason's first officer aboard the sailing ship *Covenant*. He also functions as the ship's main navigator. David at first has little contact with Shuan, but notes that he is pleasant enough during the rare times he is not drinking. When he drinks, however, he is cruel and physically violent—mostly to the ship's cabin boy, Ransome. One night, after Ransome brings Shuan a dirty piece of dishware, Shuan beats the boy so viciously that he dies. After he realizes what he has done, Shuan becomes haunted and barely able to grasp reality. Shuan is killed during the crew's assault on the roundhouse against David and Alan Breck Stewart. Because of this, the *Covenant* is navigated incompetently through the Torran Rocks, and is wrecked on a reef.

Alan Breck Stewart

Alan Breck Stewart is a Highlander who serves the heads of the Stewart clan in Appin. He is described as small in stature and rather fancily dressed, with a pockmarked face that was the result of smallpox. However, he proves himself to be both tough and a skilled fighter. A fugitive from English law because of his desertion from the army and his support of the Jacobite rebellion, Alan lives primarily in France. However, he makes periodic trips to and from Scotland to collect rents from loyal clan members for their exiled chieftain. While waiting in a small boat for his transport back to France, Alan and his clansmen are struck by the *Covenant*. Through luck and agility, Alan manages to survive the collision and climb aboard the *Covenant*. This is where he meets David Balfour, and the two become close companions and friends during their adventures.

James Stewart

James Stewart, also known as James of the Glens, is the functioning head of the Stewart clan in Appin. He is also a kinsman of Alan Breck Stewart, and the person Alan turns to after he and David are suspected of killing Colin Roy Campbell. James agrees to help, although he warns the two that he must also publicly condemn them for his own safety and the safety of his family. David and Alan discover days later that James has been arrested as an accomplice in the murder.

Mrs. Stewart

James Stewart's wife, Mrs. Stewart, is a kind woman who offers David her thanks for helping Alan and the Stewart clan. She later sends Alan and David all the money she can spare to help them escape.

Torrance

Torrance is Mister Rankeillor's clerk, and helps participate in the plan to trick Ebenezer into admitting his part in David's kidnapping.

Themes

Justice

One of the main themes running through *Kidnapped* is the idea of justice, or the execution of what is right and fair, particularly in response to past wrongs. It serves as the driving force for many of the characters' actions, although their interpretations of justice vary widely, and some contradict each other. For David, justice means exposing his uncle's evil plot and claiming his rightful inheritance. For Ebenezer, justice means holding onto the estate that was relinquished to him by his brother as part of an agreement between them. For Alan, justice means the death of Colin Roy Campbell, the man responsible for evicting his brethren from their ancestral lands. For the Campbell family and other agents of the king, justice means the arrest and execution of those involved in Campbell's murder.

Related to this theme is the recurring idea that the justice system, as it exists in the real world, is imperfect. For example, although Alan and David are innocent of the murder of Colin Roy Campbell, Alan is certain that they would be convicted of the crime, since the judge and jury—sure to be made up almost entirely of members of the Campbell clan— would be looking for vengeance wherever they could find it. Similarly, although David has a legal right to claim the house of Shaws, Mister Rankeillor knows that dealing with the court, and having to prove David's identity, would take much time and work. For this reason, they devise the plan to get Ebenezer to confess his part in the kidnapping, and then get him to reach an agreement without the need for courts.

Exile and Homesickness

The theme of exile is central to both David's story and the larger story of the people of the Jacobite Highlander clans. At the beginning of the novel, David is essentially exiled from his family home, much like the many Highlanders he later encounters. His circumstances—being denied his rightful lands and set adrift in the world—mirror those of Alan Breck Stewart, Charles Stewart, and many others. For all of them, homesickness drives their actions, for better or worse. David uses his desire to return home as a source of strength when faced with a daunting journey. Alan, who could remain safe in France, returns periodically to his homeland in Scotland even though it means risking imprisonment and death. Cluny Macpherson, a fugitive chieftain exiled from his ancestral lands, lives in hiding in modest conditions just so he can remain near his home. Many of the novel's characters have an intimate connection to and understanding of their home environment; even the blind robber David encounters on Mull, Duncan Mackiegh, can identify and describe every element of his surroundings by sound and memory.

In contrast, Ebenezer is an example of emotional exile; although he remains in his family's estate, he has shut himself off from his family and the surrounding community. No one in Cramond has a kind word to say about him, and Jennet Clouston even curses him in front of David. The dilapidated state of the house of Shaws indicates that although Ebenezer lives there, he knows in his heart that it is not his rightful home.

Topics for Further Study

- Music and song play a subtle but important role throughout *Kidnapped*. Different tunes serve as secret signals between clansmen, the singing of certain songs proves insulting or complimentary depending upon the circumstances, and a pipe-playing contest ultimately resolves a conflict between Alan

Breck Stewart and Robin Oig. Research some of the traditional Scottish songs mentioned in *Kidnapped*, and write an essay about their importance in Scottish culture. Why do different clans have their own songs? What topics and themes do the songs focus on? How might these songs help a listener better understand the Scottish people?

- In *Kidnapped*, Stevenson uses dialect and Scottish Gaelic-flavored word choices to convey the unique speech of his characters. Go through the book and create your own glossary of difficult terms, writing down the word or phrase as Stevenson uses it and then defining it in plain, modern English. Use your library, the Internet, or other available resources to research any terms that are difficult to figure out.

- David Balfour is from the Scottish Lowlands, but spends much of *Kidnapped* traveling across the Highlands. Using a map and other geographical resources, compare the Scottish Highlands and Lowlands in a short report. Where is the boundary between the two? What makes the two areas different from a geographical standpoint? How do you think geography may have played a role in the formation of separate Highland and Lowland cultures?

- In *Kidnapped*, David Balfour is taken by force from his homeland, to be sent to the Americas and sold as a slave. Although David is ultimately spared this fate, millions of real-life captives were not. Watch the Steven Spielberg film *Amistad* (1997), based on the true story of an enslaved group of West Africans who took control of their captors' ship but ended up as prisoners in America as their fates were decided by the Supreme Court. Write a report comparing the two depictions. How are the conditions and treatment aboard the *Amistad* different from what is experienced by David Balfour? How are the captives' legal difficulties similar to those faced by David in the Highlands?

Journey to Manhood

David's journey from Queensferry to the Highlands and back again is not just geographical; it is also emotional. He begins the novel as an arrogant boy with little understanding of the world he inhabits. Along the way, he learns courage, survival skills, the history of his family and his culture, and the importance of humility. This growth is first seen when he overcomes his fear of Captain Hoseason and his men, and chooses to warn Alan that the ship's crew is planning to murder him. David also experiences several other landmark events often associated with the passage into manhood. For example, he learns to fire a pistol and fends off the ship's crew alongside Alan. Soon thereafter, he becomes stranded on what he believes to be a desolate island, and must survive by his own wits for several days. Later, he holds true to his convictions about gambling in spite of temptation when he and Alan stay with Cluny Macpherson. Most importantly, he chooses to act selflessly and risk his own safety so that he might help Alan escape Scotland.

Historical Fiction

Kidnapped is an example of historical fiction, in which an author tells a fictional tale set within a realistically rendered historical time and place. For this novel, the time and place is eighteenth-century Scotland. Often, the author weaves actual historical events and people into the fictional narrative. Stevenson uses several real-life figures in *Kidnapped*, including Alan Breck Stewart, James Stewart, Robin Oig, and Colin Roy Campbell. Although he uses artistic license in his depictions of these characters, they are largely based upon available descriptions from various historical sources. In addition, one of the most significant occurrences in the novel—the murder of Colin Roy Campbell—is based closely on true events. Sometimes an author uses historical events to mirror or resonate with the happenings within the story. In *Kidnapped*, Stevenson uses the plight of Jacobite Highlanders during the eighteenth century as a direct parallel to his tale of a young man's attempt to reclaim his rightful estate.

Local Color

"Local color" is the term used to describe literary work that emphasizes the details of a specific location. This may include realistic descriptions of geography and plants and animals living in the area, as well as dialogue or narration that captures the speaking rhythms, dialect, and diction used by local people. Works of local color may also focus on the beliefs or customs of the people of the region, as well as their history. The term is applied most frequently to American authors such as Mark Twain, William Faulkner, and John Steinbeck. Stevenson uses these same local color techniques throughout *Kidnapped*. Nearly every character, including the narrator, speaks in a dialect unusual—and sometimes potentially indecipherable —to American readers. Stevenson also spends a great deal of time describing the route taken by David across Scotland, naming every landmark and describing the topography and vegetation found in the area. Finally, Stevenson introduces many elements of Scottish custom and culture to David, and by extension, to his readers.

The Jacobite Risings and Aftermath

One of the most significant events in the history of relations between Scotland and England occurred in 1688, when King James II of England—who also served as ruler of Scotland and Ireland—was overthrown and replaced by his Dutch son-in-law, William III. One of the main reasons for the overthrow of James II was his religion, Roman Catholicism, which had become very unpopular in England during the previous century and had led to the formation of the separate Church of England. For this reason, William III, who was not Catholic but Protestant, became the new king, and the laws were changed so that the royal family line passed down only through the Protestant portion of the family.

This development was not well received by many in Ireland or in Highland Scotland, because Roman Catholicism was the prevailing religion and James II himself was the leader of the House of Stewarts (the clan from which Alan Breck Stewart and James of the Glens hail in *Kidnapped*). Many clans rebelled against the new king, demanding that James II or his descendants be returned to the throne. These rebels became known as "Jacobites," after the Latin word for "James." Two different rebellions occurred, in 1715 and in 1745; the second was led by Charles Edward Stewart, half brother to James of the Glens, and its failure led to his exile in France.

In response to this rebellion, King George II of England ordered his agents in the Highlands to strip the rebellious clans of their ancestral lands, which would come under control of the king and could be distributed or rented as he saw fit. Some chieftains fled to France, while others simply remained in the Highlands and lived as fugitives. Despite the efforts of the king, many members of the Jacobite clans continued to support their exiled chieftains, secretly aiding them with money or shelter as needed.

The Appin Murder

One of the key events in *Kidnapped* is the murder of the king's agent, known as the Red Fox. In 1752, Colin Roy Campbell—known as the Red Fox because of his hair color—was working on behalf of King George II to remove rebellious Highland chieftains from their estates. He claimed the land in the name of the king and was largely disliked by the members of the clans he evicted, which included the Stewart clan. In the days or weeks leading up to Campbell's death, Alan Breck Stewart was reportedly heard to ask publicly, "Who will bring me the skin of the Red Fox?"

Compare & Contrast

- **1750s:** Scottish Jacobite clans suffer after an unsuccessful rebellion against the British monarchy.

  1880s: Scotland and England together operate as a formidable center of world industry.

  Today: The Scottish National Party, whose goal is to gain status as a nation independent from England, maintains a minority control of the Scottish government.

- **1750s:** In the Scottish Highlands, the kilt—a traditional skirt-like garment worn by men—is banned by the British government, as are decorative fabric patterns specific to certain Highland clans.

  1880s: A reawakening of interest in Scottish culture, and an easing of tensions between England and Scotland, allow the kilt to be adopted as a symbol of traditional Scotland.

  Today: The kilt enjoys a limited resurgence both in and out of Scotland as a fashionable clothing item for men.

- **1750s:** Popular English literature consists of works like Henry Fielding's *Tom Jones* (1749), a comic novel broken down into several smaller books.

1880s: Popular literature is dominated by periodicals that publish works of serial fiction, spread across multiple issues and filled with cliffhangers to maintain reader interest for the next installment.

Today: Popular television shows such as *Lost* follow a format similar to serial fiction of the past, often ending each episode with a twist or cliffhanger.

On May 14, 1752, while traveling along a road in Appin, Campbell was killed by a single shot. No other members of his party were fired upon or injured. Although no one could identify the shooter, and James Stewart—the putative head of the Stewart clan during his brother's exile—was seen by witnesses far from the scene of the crime, he was arrested for playing a part in the murder. Although there was no evidence against him, James was found guilty by a jury composed mostly of members of the Campbell clan, and was executed by hanging on November 8, 1752. His decomposing body was then put on display to send a message to other Jacobite rebels, and remained on display for three years. No other parties, including Alan Breck Stewart, were ever arrested or tried for the murder.

Critical Overview

When *Kidnapped* was published in 1886, Stevenson was already established as a successful writer of popular fiction for children and adults. His novel *Treasure Island* (1883) was both critically acclaimed and a best-seller, and his novella *Strange Case of Dr. Jekyll and Mr. Hyde* (1886) proved his ability to craft more adult fare. Because *Kidnapped* was largely considered an adventure novel for boys, much like *Treasure Island*, it is not surprising that many reviewers compared the two, with *Treasure Island* often coming up the favorite. An unsigned reviewer from the *St. James Gazette* writes of the book, "Its incidents are not so uniformly thrilling [as *Treasure Island*] ... yet *Kidnapped* is excellent from end to end." R. H. Hutton, comparing the two in a review for *The Spectator*, notes, "*Kidnapped* is not so ideal a story of external adventure as *Treasure Island*." However, he also notes that *Kidnapped* has "perhaps even more of the qualities proper to all true literature." Author Arthur Conan Doyle expresses similar sentiments writing for the *National Review*: "*Treasure Island* is perhaps the better story, while *Kidnapped* may have the longer lease of life as being an excellent and graphic sketch of the state of the Highlands after the last Jacobite insurrection." Author Henry James, in an article for *The Century Magazine*, calls the novel "the finest of his longer stories," and considers the character of Alan Breck to be "a masterpiece."

Although critics at the time suggested that *Kidnapped* might outlast *Treasure Island* as enduring literature, the novel has remained less popular than Stevenson's earlier tale of treasure and pirates. Even worse, despite the continuous popularity of his books, Stevenson's entire body of work was all but ignored by academics and literary scholars during the first half of the twentieth century. In recent decades, Stevenson has finally been acknowledged for his contributions to English literature, and *Kidnapped* remains extraordinarily popular among modern readers both young and old.

What Do I Read Next?

- Stevenson's *Catriona* (1893), originally published in the United States as *David Balfour*, picks up where *Kidnapped* ends. It continues the story of David and Alan Breck, focusing largely on their efforts to prove James Stewart innocent of the Appin Murder.

- *Treasure Island* (1883), Stevenson's first novel, is one of the best-known and most frequently adapted adventure tales ever written. In it, a poor young man discovers a pirate's treasure map and sets out to claim the booty, unknowingly bringing with him a bloodthirsty, one-legged pirate named Long John Silver who intends to keep the treasure for himself.

- *Waverley* (1814) by Sir Walter Scott is one of the earliest examples of historical fiction. The book takes place in Scotland during the Jacobite Rising of 1745—just six years before *Kidnapped*—and like Stevenson's novel, it offers a sympathetic view of the Jacobite Highlanders and their struggles.

- Patrick O'Brian's historical novel *Master and Commander* (1970) offers seafaring adventure of a different sort than *Kidnapped*. In the novel, the first in a series of over twenty books, a naval captain is given command of a new ship and hires on a physician friend as his naval surgeon. As in *Kidnapped*, the adventures of the captain and his crew are interwoven into actual historical events from the turn of the nineteenth century.

- *Twenty Thousand Leagues Under the Sea* (1872) by Jules Verne is a different kind of sea adventure. In it, a crew hired by the United States government takes to the sea in pursuit of a mysterious monster that turns out to be a technological marvel: a submarine piloted by the enigmatic Captain Nemo. Three crew members are taken prisoner by Nemo and travel the seas of the world, experiencing adventures ranging from an attack by a giant squid to a visit to the undersea ruins of Atlantis.

- Daniel Defoe's novel *Robinson Crusoe* (1719) is the "true autobiography" of a sailor who becomes shipwrecked alone on an island off the coast of South America. During his twenty-eight years on the island, he encounters cannibals and mutineers, and befriends a native man known only as "Friday," named after the day Crusoe first meets him.

Sources

Campbell, Joseph, *The Hero with a Thousand Faces*, MJF Books, 1949, pp. 59, 97, 246.

Doyle, Arthur Conan, "Mr. Stevenson's Methods in Fiction," in the *National Review*, January, 1890. Reprinted in *A Peculiar Gift: Nineteenth Century Writings on Books for Children*, edited by Lance Salway, Kestrel Books, 1976, pp. 391-403.

Hutton, R. H., Review of *Kidnapped*, in *The Spectator*, Vol. LIX, No. 3030, July 24, 1886, pp. 990-91, reprinted in *Nineteenth Century Literature Criticism*, edited by Laurie Lanzen Harris and Sheila Fitzgerald, Vol. 5., Gale Research, 1984, p. 400.

James, Henry, "Robert Louis Stevenson," in *The Century Magazine*, Vol. XXXV, No. 6, April 1888, reprinted in his *Partial Portraits*, Macmillan and Co., 1888, pp. 137-174.

Review of *Kidnapped*, in the *St. James Gazette*, Vol. XIII, July 19, 1886, reprinted in *Robert Louis Stevenson: The Critical Heritage*, edited by Paul Maixner, Routledge & Kegan Paul, 1981, pp. 233-235.

The Robert Louis Stevenson Website, http://dinamico2.unibg.it/rls/films-kidn.htm (accessed June 3, 2009).

Stevenson, Robert Louis, *Kidnapped*, revised edition, Penguin Books, 2007.

————, Letter written to Robert Stevenson, January 25, 1886, in *The Letters of Robert Louis Stevenson*, available from the University of Adelaide Library of Electronic Texts Collection, http://ebooks.adelaide.edu.au/s/stevenson/robert_lou (accessed June 3, 2009).

Further Reading

Herman, Arthur., *How the Scots Invented the Modern World*, Crown, 2001.

> This history book offers a unique hypothesis: that the modern world was largely shaped by the ideas and actions of the great Scottish thinkers, inventors, and political figures of the eighteenth and nineteenth centuries.

Harman, Claire, *Myself and the Other Fellow: A Life of Robert Louis Stevenson*, HarperCollins, 2005.

> This biography comprehensively examines every aspect of the author's short but productive life.

Tranter, Nigel, *The Wallace: The Compelling 13th Century Story of William Wallace*, Hodder & Stoughton, 1975.

> This historical novel focuses on a legendary Scot who lived centuries before the Jacobite Risings. Tranter's tale offers a realistic portrayal of the legendary Wallace's military accomplishments as leader of Scottish resistance forces fighting English soldiers during Scotland's war for independence.

Menikoff, Barry, *Narrating Scotland: The*

Imagination of Robert Louis Stevenson, University of South Carolina Press, 2005.

> In this nonfiction work, Menikoff argues that Stevenson's varied writings, often dismissed as genre work, served a single unified purpose: to capture the experience, culture, and history of the Scottish people and preserve it for the sake of posterity.